BEGINNING YOUR MYSTIC JOURNEY

MODERN MYSTIC

Finding Your Mystic Self

Made with love by the team at

FIVE MILE

Alex, Niki, Rocco, Graham, Jacqui, Claire, Amy & Lyndal

Five Mile,
the publishing division
of Regency Media
www.fivemile.com.au

First published 2022

It is the author's study and experience that has led to the content of this book. It is an amalgamation of the author's interpretation of information from both contemporary and ancient sources.

Printed in China 5 4 3 2 1

CONTENTS

WHEN A LAKE IS STILL, THE LIGHT OF THE MOON CAN REFLECT CLEARLY UPON THE WATER

Welcome

If you generally wish to feel a little more peaceful in your life, then you already qualify as a mystic. The search is over. You do not need to join an ashram or monastery, start composing poetry, ethereal symphonies or believe in anything that is not believable to you in order to connect with your mystic self.

All that we can do within this edition, is guide you through a series of easy-to-use practices that will allow you to see your mystic self more clearly. Informed through ancient traditions, the techniques that you are about to learn hold the potential to help abate within you debilitating states of restlessness, doubt, fear, worry, shame, fatigue and alienation.

Safely and gently, we will walk with you through these wisdom teachings until you truly feel that you have found your inner mystic.

In this book, you will learn to:

- Understand an inclusive definition of being a mystic and what it means to be on a mystical path
- Locate and befriend your Centre
- Understand the role of the lonely teacher
- Quieten your mind chatter
- Understand the importance of breathing
- Revitalise your spirit with water
- Reset your thymus
- Understand the role of the vagus nerve on your mystic journey
- Dowse via body swaying
- Earth/Ground yourself
- Learn to identify and responsibly clear stagnant energy and fortify your auric field
- Locate and clear your seven major chakras
- Disentangle from non life-affirming energies

We are happy to be on this journey with you, dear mystic. Now — take a deep breath from your feet and let's go.

Mystic words

Below is a list of words that you will come across in this book:

AURIC FIELD

The egg-shaped field that surrounds you. It is comprised of sheaths that are connected with your major chakras. It is possible to clear distortion from your aura before it adversely manifests into your physical body.

CENTRE

That place inside yourself that is always safe, clear, strong and filled by beauty and light.

CHAKRA

From Sanskrit, the word chakra means 'wheel' or 'spinning disk'. Your chakras facilitate the flow of energy in and out of your body. Their health is critical to your health on every level.

DOWSING

Dowsing is a technique that utilises a tool to detect or reveal information.

EARTHING/GROUNDING

A remedial technique that corrects and maintains your healthy electrical connectivity with the Earth. Science now acknowledges its effectiveness in reducing inflammation in the body.

MUDRĀ

A symbolic gesture. Certain hand mudrās can be used to clear non life-affirming energies from you.

MYSTIC

- Some one who seeks to find unity
- Some one who seeks to feel peaceful inside
- Some one who is remembering more often that they are enough always, in every way

MYSTICAL PATH

What you have embarked upon through magnetising this book into your world.

THYMUS

The endocrine gland that is connected with your body's immunity. It is governed by your heart chakra and lives within the frontside of your body between your heart and throat.

TRANSMUTATIONAL FIRE

To transmute means to change one thing into something else. You can use transmutational fire (literal and/or figurative) to ensure the correct disposal of non life-affirming energies.

VAGUS NERVE

Your 10th cranial nerve that originates from your brain stem. It is connected with your eyes, ears, nose, speech, throat, lungs, heart, liver and, very importantly, your gut and digestive system.

What is a mystic?

When you think of a mystic, do you see a spiritual teacher hovering above the ground, legs crossed in lotus pose, dressed only in an orange cloth? Or maybe you see a hermit-like recluse with a halo-like glow around their head?

From a historical context, many mystical figures have lived within a powerful state of full devotion to God or their chosen deity. Here is a short list of some known traditional mystics that you may like to investigate further:

- Hildegard of Bingen
- Rumi
- Teresa of Ávila
- Saint Francis of Assisi
- Joan of Arc
- Pierre Teilhard de Chardin

If it feels natural for you to follow a path similar to any of the above figures, that is both inspiring and amazing to us all here in your Modern Mystic team. Our world shines infinitely brighter when spirits like you come and help things evolve in our world through new forms of amazing music and art.

But, an even more potent force than great artistry comes from you beginning to notice that, on a more regular basis, you are feeling better, clearer and gradually more positive about each present moment and the future.

What does it mean to be on a mystical path?

The traditional definition of being upon a mystical path is:

- Someone who innately believes in truths that lie outside intellectual comprehension
- Someone who prays, contemplates and surrenders in order to merge with and be of service to their deity

Our definition is a little different. We have reconfigured it so that no one can ever feel excluded:

- Someone who seeks to find unity
- Someone who seeks to feel peaceful inside
- Someone who is remembering more often, and all the time, that they are enough, always, in every way

Whether perceiving the mystical path in the traditional sense or what we redefine it as, there is one other thing that true mystics have in common. This is the ability to keep their hearts and minds open to trusting that no matter how hard or bad things may seem, everything always, eventually, works out not only for the highest interests of every person individually, but also builds towards a collective greater good.

Below you will read a little more about a mystic named Rumi and learn exactly which part of you may have just voiced scepticism that things always work out for the best.

Understand that your doubts are normal and healthy. But, when doubts and worries get too big, they then can become some of the strongest boundaries that keep you separated from finding your mystic self.

As with everything, it is totally up to you which of these practices you opt to adapt into your life.

What we can learn from Rumi's mystic pathway

From our earlier list of known mystics, the Persian poet, Rumi, was deeply afflicted with very intense feelings of grief, despair and emptiness. It is a speculative hypothesis, but possible that Rumi's son ordered an honour-killing upon Shams, the most-loved companion of Rumi. With or without this great trauma, Rumi didn't begin to really find his mystical self until his mid–late 30s.

Whether Rumi's beloved Shams was murdered or not, as Rumi grieved for Shams, it is feasible that during this hard time, Rumi was not filled by the belief that life was working out for his highest good. It would perhaps have been understandable if such a painful life experience broke Rumi and left him bitter, or seeking vengefully to impose his own sense of justice or punishment; 'to right a great wrong'.

Gratefully, instead, Rumi used his freewill to heal and let go of the bitterness and remorse from his past. If you feel drawn to explore any of his Work, you will understand more fully the great gift of Rumi's mystic pathway.

We share this to help you see the immense power that you hold to positively change our world. Through one simple decision, you too can choose to heal and release all traumas from your past.

Just like Rumi, it may take you a little while to steadfastly anchor yourself into alignment with your mystic self. Trust that this is totally fine and normal. Please always be gentle and loving with yourself.

It is time now to shift the destructive narrative that runs in so much of our world today. You are a crucial link in this process. We get that Earth at times can feel like a confusing, cruel and painful place to be. But we are now in an age to change this together. Activate your power, light-worker. The narrative of hatred and revenge—to make, feed and highlight what divides rather than what unites people—is not inline with your mystic journey.

THE MYSTICAL PATH LOSES OBSESSION WITH 'I AM RIGHT AND YOU ARE WRONG' — THE MYSTICAL PATH IS CONCERNED WITH PEACE AND UNITY

BECOMING YOUR MYSTIC SELF

Befriending your Centre

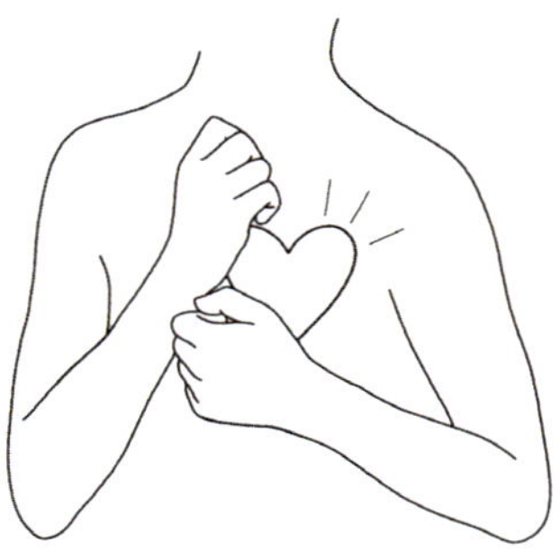

You are born in an age that sees many influences (and influencers) trying to continually compel you to act in a certain way, buy things you don't actually need and doubt your intrinsic worth and naturally evolving beauty.

As you make stronger contact with your mystic self, you will learn to trust that it is entirely in your power to remove all permission that you have given for these projections and distractions to cloud the uniquely perfect expression of who, what, why and how you really are.

Finding your Centre

In a sphere there is one distinct, central point. In you, there is also a singular, central space. If you have ever been into a holy sanctuary or a designated space of worship such as a temple, a mosque or a church, you may have noticed that there is generally a centrally located, dedicated sacred space.

Upon this altar there may be scriptures that have been recorded and passed through ages to help people on their way. There may also be a polished goblet, like a holy grail, that directs awareness to our hearts. There may be beautiful feathers or rocks, crystals or other significant objects infused with special meanings.

From today, if becoming or re-becoming a mystic feels true for you inside your bones, then you now need to locate that central space inside you. It is not hard to do. It costs no money and nothing can ever interfere with your Centre once you have decided that you are ready to live all of your life from it.

Some people call this space God/dess or Buddha-nature. Others feel it as calm silence. We call it Yom. You can call it anything you like, or nothing at all. The only important thing is that you make connection with this space, now.

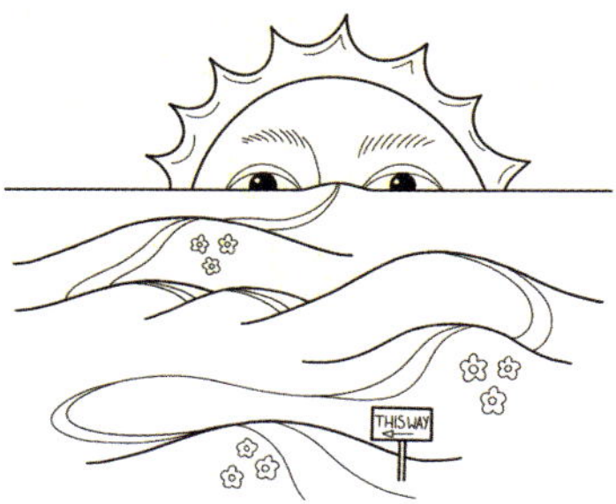

Creating your Centre

Close your eyes, take a deep breath and imagine a calm place inside you. It can be big or little, multi-roomed or just one bright flame. You can make homes for your totem animal friends in this space. It can have a massive waterfall. You can do anything and everything you like. Just make sure that there is one centrally sanctified space where you can go that is aglow with the most luminous radiance.

The light that you will see or feel in your Centre is of the same quality that people report upon once they have returned from a near-death experience.

Your lit Centre is the symbol of how potent and powerful you really are, with or without a new pair of shoes or an updated phone. Your luminous Centre, in essence, is what every Sage or Perfect Master is.

Your Centre is your mystic self.

It is your true home.

BECOMING YOUR MYSTIC SELF:

MIND

The lonely teacher

The id, the ego and the super-ego

Early psychoanalytical modelling divided the brain into two categories: the conscious and subconscious mind. In the subconscious mind, there are three main parts: the 'id', the 'ego' and the 'super-ego'.

The id maintains the instinctual, primal aspect of our minds; the part of us that makes demands. Often, the demands from the id or dual-self nature are self-serving, aggressive and/or sexual.

The ego is like a diplomat or a mediating go-between, which runs the demands from the id through a 'reality-metre'.

The super-ego brings a moral conscience into the equation, which further modifies the actions that would be taken to satisfy the id's demands.

For people trained in traditional models of psychoanalysis, psychiatry or psychology, models akin to the id, ego and super-ego may remain relevant and helpful. For us, we opt to present you with a simplified version:

The primary or authentic self = **the mystic self**
The secondary self/selves = **fragmented perceptions of the lonely teacher (ego or dual-self nature)**

Why the lonely teacher?

The primary reason we refer to the dual-self nature as the lonely teacher is because this aspect of us will do anything to separate and isolate us from life. Your mystic self does not operate in this way. Your mystic self will always focus on what unites and connects life. Understanding your lonely teacher is therefore very important as it is the greatest obstacle and saboteur to you being your mystic self.

Your lonely teacher is:

- The part of your mind that holds onto grudges
- Your self-critical voice. The one that thinks your butt is too big, that your arms aren't toned, that you are failing in the world because not enough people liked your social media post
- The part of your conditioned being that feels afraid and isolated, the part that traps you into feeling lonely
- What always focusses upon division over unity

To put it simply: the lonely teacher is why it sounds hard to believe that things always, eventually, work out for the best.

We could hear your lonely teacher brewing up opposition and reasons for your assured failure in finding your mystic self as soon as you opened this book. And that is totally expected. It may also be one of the reasons why you are here, allowing these words to remind you of your true self. That is, you feel tired in many ways from the insecurity that comes from the lonely teacher's perpetual onslaught of self-criticism, negative judgment and preoccupation with escalating things unnecessarily. The lonely teacher's basic mechanism is to keep you away from feeling the closeness you seek with other hearts. It is the essence of all imbalanced power on this planet.

To function in this world, to even get out of bed in the morning, all of us need a little ego. However, most of our world's current population could benefit from more soul or 'primary essence' and less psycho-drama. The next sections explain some simple ways to help quieten your lonely teacher when it gets a little too loud.

Questioning your lonely teacher — Ramana Maharshi

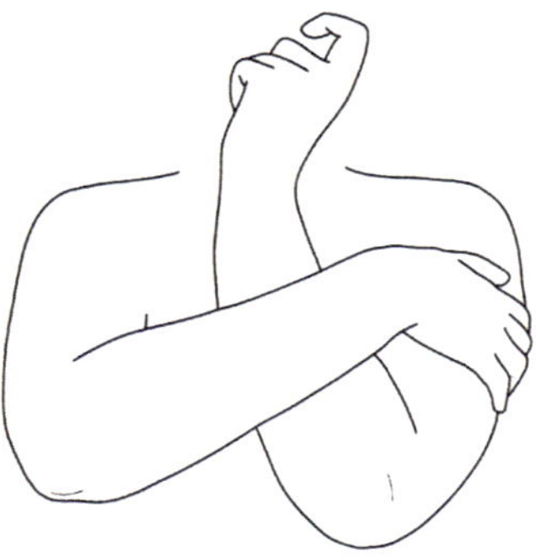

Though Ramana Maharshi is more frequently referred to as a saint or a sage, with our redefinition of mystic, he (and many others) could easily be considered a mystic. You may find one of his self-inquiry techniques helpful at this point on your mystic path. Next time a negative thought about yourself arises, lovingly ask: 'who am I?' or 'who said that?'

As soon as you have consciously directed your attention in this way, you will immediately recognise that it is not your mystic (authentic) self speaking, but rather your lonely teacher. Your primary, true, authentic, mystic self quite literally never focusses on anything that is not oriented towards loving kindness.

Try it. Next time you realise you are feeling insecure because your lonely teacher has been chanting negative thoughts through your mind such as 'your jeans don't look great on your legs', smile and ask: 'who said that?'

Quietening your mind chatter

If you have ever lived with a puppy, you will know that you must stay patient and kind whilst your puppy learns not to chew your shoes and toilet rolls.

Your lonely teacher (ego) is in some ways like a puppy. It may not yet know any better than to talk to you at all hours of the night about the way that person at the station stared at you, an upcoming deadline, an embarrassing situation from years before, the list goes on. It needs your gentle patience and kindness to learn when and how to be silent.

Over the past couple of decades in my clinical practice, there have been a significant number of people who have been able to wean away from drugs and dramatically improve their sleep by using this slightly modified ancient 'hum-sah' breathing practice. If you have been afflicted by mind chatter at bedtime or any other time, we trust that this simple technique may prove to be of similar help to you.

If you tend to wake during the night, it could be helpful to put some little reminder, perhaps a smooth stone, in or near your bed to help remind you to do this practice when you prematurely wake.

HUM ... SAH

Follow these steps to help silence mind chatter. It is a wonderful technique to use before you go to sleep each night.

STEP 1: BREATHE IN

When you breathe in, simply think the whole time that you are breathing in the sound 'HUM'.

STEP 2: HOLD

Now, instead of breathing in a cycle of two (in then out), you are going to establish a new rhythm of breathing in a sequence of three: in ... hold ... out.

In this middle 'hold' space, you are going to peacefully count for however long feels good. Never strain or force this step. Whilst you count, not only is there no space for the lonely teacher to resume with any dominating noise, your super-wise body is also being gifted the opportunity to self-regulate and prepare for rest.

STEP 3: BREATHE OUT

When you breathe out, simply think the whole time that you are breathing out the sound 'SAH'.

Be sure you are breathing in this cycle of three in a way that is deeply comfortable for you. That said, it can be helpful, especially with the first couple of breaths, if you focus on making the out breath just a little longer than your inhalation. You will learn more as to why this is of extra benefit when we get to the vagus nerve section.

Another useful tip is to only use your nose, not your mouth if this is possible, and to make sure that you huff out the stale air from the very bottom part of your lungs. If you find the puppy is running off with your shoe, just become aware of which part of your breathing you are up to, and peacefully, without self-condemnation, return to hum-sah-ing.

BECOMING YOUR MYSTIC SELF:

BODY

WE ARE ABLE TO
REMEMBER OUR
INNATE FREEDOM
WHEN THE
ARTIFICIAL
MECHANISM
KNOWN AS TIME
IS TEMPORARILY
TRANSCENDED

Take a breath

There is a science that has been estranged and alienated from our lives. Through this separation, we, the people of this world, have grown restless inside.

In Latin, *spirare* (pronounced spear-ra-ray) means breath. Our word spirit comes from this, *spiritus*, to breathe.

Whenever we get stuck inside a thought-loop in our head, we generally short circuit our breathing. As soon as this happens, the clarity of all reflection becomes blurry, chopped up and hectic. Your mind's peace is gone.

Wherever you are, breathe in your next breath as if the air is entering you through your feet, not your face. As you draw this breath up through your body, try to use your nose not your mouth. It is okay for now if this is not possible.

Make sure your breath is spacious. There is no hurry here; no time device measuring you. You are not running behind. There is no one in the sky about to strike you down. There is nothing you are missing out on. Right here, right now, you are exactly where, how and who you are meant to be.

When you are ready, breathe in another time through your feet. Feel how in doing this your tummy moves. Then, instead of breathing out straight away, hold this breath comfortably, maybe just to the count of three or four (it is okay if it is less or more), whatever feels free of any strain for you.

Then, when you are ready, either in silence or with sound, let your breath go. Make sure you huff out that last bit of dead air from the bottom of your lungs like you may have done during your 'hum-sah' breathing. Direct your breath with thought into the ground.

Now, only when you are ready, let's begin aligning your body for the vital residency of your mystic self.

Revitalise your spirit with water

Viktor Schauberger devoted his life to understanding water. He is quoted as saying:

> "The true foundation of all culture is the knowledge and understanding of water."

He also made a prediction that the action of forcing water through linear piping would result in the disintegration of society — quite a strong sentiment.

It may seem like a weird thing to include in a book about mysticism, but if your goal is to have longevity and peace upon your mystical path, mindful breathing and water are the foundation stones upon which you must start.

Ways to bring water into your spiritual practice

RELAX THE WATER YOU DRINK

Observations have found that water's molecules cluster more tightly together when pressurised through piping.

Knowing that our body is about 70 per cent water, think about how you feel when you have just been forced into a tight deadline situation, and then how you feel after you have been allowed to chill out for a little while. Your body is given the opportunity and space it needs to unwind and reset. It is exactly the same for the water you drink. Allowing water to rest and restructure is a wonderful, simple way to make drinking water a more deeply quenching, calming and spiritual experience.

TREATING WATER AS SACRED

Traditional Indian culture has been aware for some time of the importance of treating water as sacred. They have a practice whereby water is decanted into copper vessels and left overnight before consuming. In some households, a fresh flower or crystal is placed on top of the re-energising water.

A simple and healing way to sacredly drink water is to source some coloured glass bottles and decant your tap water into them. To make this even more beneficial, leave the water in direct sunlight for a little while to solar charge your water before drinking it. One hour can be enough. To further enhance the quality of your water, you may like to research the power of words upon water and/or utilise images of Masaru Emoto's incredibly beautiful and life-promoting water crystals.

Slow down for the few seconds it takes for the water to decant into your glass or bottle. Spend this time infusing the water with positive thoughts, feelings, prayers or intentions. You could try saying from your heart: 'thank you water, I love you'. Then, when you drink the water, this thought or statement becomes a part of you.

Another intentional prayer-form that we often structure into our water, is for all life on Earth to have free and limitless access to truly safe, living water.

FIGURE OUT YOUR WEIGHT–WATER RATIO

The recommendation to drink eight glasses of water a day always seemed pretty arbitrary to us. So we were grateful when we were taught this helpful equation.

Here is the simple maths: your body weight in kilograms multiplied by 25. This will give you a figure in millilitres that you need to clear basic metabolic waste from your system in a 24-hour period.

For example:

A person who weighs 60 kg will need
1.5 L of water per 24-hour period (60 x 25 = 1,500 ml).

If you are fasting or flushing toxins from your body, or if you are taking a lot of medications, drinking lots of caffeine or alcohol, or you are involved in a profession or pasttime that sees you sweating a lot, this amount of water may need to be modified. We are all unique, and it is perhaps the most important part of being on your mystic path that you listen to your inner guidance, always.

If you are nowhere near the quantity that you calculate, do not try to achieve this too quickly. Simply start increasing your intake little by little each day.

FILTERING AND RE-ENERGISING WATER

Depending on your circumstances, researching and possibly investing in a water filtration and/or restructuring device might be an option for you. After doing some research, you may also find that you can make your own restructuring tools. Anything that replicates the way water moves in nature, swirling and circling, will enhance your water's quality.

Resetting your thymus

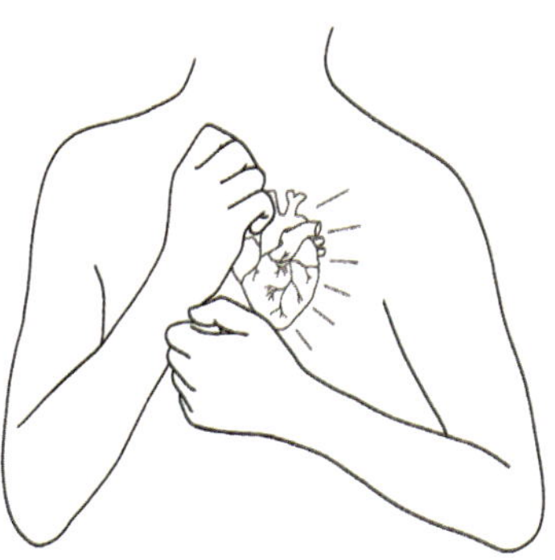

Dr John Diamond MD, passed from this world in 2021. In his book *Your Body Doesn't Lie*, he shares an important key to wellbeing called the 'thymus thump', or 'thymus tap'. It is a very simple and quick practice that you can do any time.

The thymus is a gland situated between the top of your lungs on the front midline of your body. You can locate yours by roughly measuring the middle point between your throat and your heart. It was most active when you were young, working to establish a strong immune system. After this time, however, it continues to hold a critical function, almost like a fuse box in a house.

Some examples to help you understand when you will need to reset your thymus:

- You are feeling good. Plenty of energy with a clear head. Then, someone starts talking to you. Maybe it is not too bad, or maybe it feels like a big conversation. As you part ways from this person, you realise you are not feeling so clear in your head anymore. Your energy feels flatter—you might even feel a bit scattered.
- You walk into your parent's house. The news is on. There has been a bad accident. There is an interview with an eyewitness. Their voice sounds stressed. Again, from feeling clear and energised, you begin to sense you are not feeling so great anymore.

- You find yourself listening to a politician who is avoiding answering a simple and direct question. This politician spins out many words of blame and very few of plain truth. There is a vague, dull sense within you that was not there before their noise.

The great thing is that no matter how distressed the sounds around you grow or how thick the political spin is, as you align yourself more with your mystic self, the stronger you will become and the less frequent it will be that your thymus gets disrupted.

This unshakable stability is not reserved for an elite chosen few. It is available to everyone. Plus, the energy that you put into keeping yourself clear and in alignment with your primary, mystic self gives a healing, flow-on effect to others around you. Over time, you will quite naturally become an activation portal for other people.

How to reset your thymus:

1. Tap repeatedly over your thymus.
2. At the same time, smile (this step is essential).
3. It is optional, but can sometimes speed the resetting, to simultaneously laugh out loud. This need be no more than the sound 'ha, ha, ha' as you tap and smile.

You will know when you have successfully reset your thymus by an increased clarity in your mind. Generally, resetting your thymus takes around 5–15 seconds.

We thank Dr John Diamond for this technique and his service to our world.

The vagus nerve

How can a nerve have anything to do with your mystic path? Maybe seeing its pathway will help you to better understand:

Once referred to as the pneumo (lung) – gastric (stomach) nerve, it may be a little clearer to you from this illustration, whether finding your mystic self or not, why it is so important to ensure that this nerve is free and vibrant within you.

The words 'vagabond' and 'vague' both originate from the same Latin root, *vagus*, meaning 'to wander'. If you have been so blessed as to walk upon a path through a lush rainforest or beautiful garden, you will know that the freedom from all awareness of time pressure significantly enhances such an experience.

Both vagabonds and being vague are often negatively associated. For us, looking with a different perspective, this is not always the case. With vagabonds, we chose to honour and connect these people with the lineage of spiritual pilgrims: those people who have surrendered entirely into not being bound by conventional mechanisms and constraints such as time and fixed addresses.

Likewise, when we are genuinely engaged or touched, we are not vague. The tendency to 'vague-out' (generally and simply) comes about when there is a split or disassociation between our heart and mind. Therefore, 'vaguing out' can be used as a useful reminder to check in with ourselves and reset one of the primary anatomical links between our heart and mind.

Resetting your vagus nerve

1. Find a peaceful place.
2. Become aware of the feeling of your breath moving in and out of your body.
3. In a nurturing and comfortable way, place your hands or fingers **gently** into the little nook that you find at the back of your head, in the middle, directly below your skull bone. This is the homeland of your cranial nerves. Your vagus nerve is the tenth nerve in this family of twelve. If you are unable to anchor this place yourself, please ask someone with whom you feel completely safe to cradle this part of your head for you.
4. With eyes open or closed, and very importantly without moving any other part of your face or head, turn your eyes to either the left or right.
5. Whilst contact is maintained with the origin point of your vagus nerve at the base of your skull: breathe slowly in, as if the air is entering in through the soles of your feet.
6. Calmly hold this breath for whatever time feels right for you.
7. Let go of this breath, making sure your exhalation is longer than your inhalation.
8. Repeat steps 4–7 until you either yawn or swallow. If your eyeballs begin to feel stressed, simply rest them for a little while. Also, if this more 'conscious' style of breathing begins to feel difficult, take a few breaths in whichever way feels good for you before returning to the rhythm suggested in steps 5–7.
9. Allow your mystic self to guide you as to the correct number of yawns or swallows. It can range from just one swallow through to multiple, eye-watering yawns.
10. Rest if necessary or drink some water, before moving

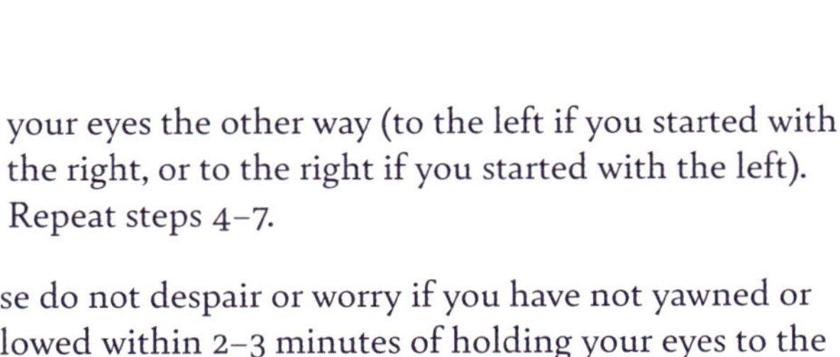

your eyes the other way (to the left if you started with the right, or to the right if you started with the left).

11. Repeat steps 4–7.

Please do not despair or worry if you have not yawned or swallowed within 2–3 minutes of holding your eyes to the side. We are committed to helping ensure that you are able to reset your vagus nerve and begin the process of strengthening its tone and vitality.

If you have been through or are having a hard time, please be very patient and kind with yourself.

Here are some other helpful vagus nerve tonification and resetting techniques. Only do those that feel right for you.

- Sing, gargle, chant, hum
- Learn the 'ujjayi' or 'ocean breath'
- Slow down your breathing
- Swish cold water over your face, or when showering, change the water to cold for little sections of time
- Familiarise yourself with the auricular (ear) access points to your vagus nerve, and use these when needed
- Ensure you are consuming the correct levels of omega 3, preferably from plant-based sources. Learn about purslane
- Keep your guts' microbiome balanced
- Meditate, or simply breathe at least once a day with mindfulness
- Self-massage
- Laugh and allow true joy to be a part of your life
- Stop trying to win approval from outside yourself
- Find out which form of exercise you enjoy and then enjoy doing it
- Listen a little better each day to your mystic self
- Breathe. Let your diaphragm fully open
- Smile more deeply
- Cultivate a joyful and accepting attitude

Developing your innate ability to dowse

Dowsing is a technique that utilises a tool to detect or reveal information. Examples include locating ley lines, faerie forts and underground water sources with metal rods or sticks made from materials such as bone or wood. You may use a pendulum or know of people who use this as a dowsing apparatus.

A modality known as kinesiology is based around muscle testing. This form of testing often utilises a person's arm as the dowsing tool to access information that can then be used to help rebalance health and wellbeing. Other people use the motion of a single or interlinked fingers.

The dowsing tool will naturally move towards the 'truer' form of the information. Say you cannot decide what to pick at a crystal shop, hovering a dowsing tool over the two crystal options will help you decide as it will naturally lean towards the better choice for you in that moment.

The great news is that a lot of people who are unable to dowse in any of the ways specified above find greater success when they use their own body as the dowsing tool.

Body swaying — your natural dowsing tool

Before we teach you how to dowse via body swaying, there are a few things that we need to make sure you understand. As with much of what you have been learning upon your mystic path, integrity and intention remain key. Therefore, dowsing is not for sourcing lotto numbers, sporting teams or winning horses. Nor is it for fantasy questions about what your boyfriend is thinking.

It is, however, an invaluable tool to use whilst you are food shopping or for checking on advice you may have been given as to the regularity and dosage amount for such helpers as herbal tinctures, flower essences, traditional herbs or magnesium supplementation. We urge you to do this in the presence of your consulting health practitioner so that you can then together establish what is actually the most supportive treatment protocol for your unique and changing physiology. Please continually and honestly refresh the preparatory steps below, particularly point 4.

Preparation for dowsing:

1. Body hydration. If you are dehydrated, it is less likely you will be able to dowse.
2. Being 'on or off'. You can start a dowsing session and 'turn off' part way through, or you can find you are 'not on' before you have started. If you find this is the case, use the thymus tap with smile as taught in the 'Resetting your thymus' section.
3. If you are experiencing strong emotions or feel unstable in your mind, now is not the best time to dowse.
4. If you have already decided what the answer should be to your question, this can corrupt the accuracy of the reading. It is therefore best that you re-establish neutrality or greater equanimity in your mind before dowsing.
5. It is preferable not to dowse directly beneath a fluorescent light.

How to body sway

Once you have satisfied the requirements specified in the preceding section, follow these four easy steps. If you are unable to stand, you can also do this from either a sitting or prone (lying flat on you back) position.

STEP 1

Stand evenly and comfortably. Then, calmly centre yourself.

STEP 2

Establish you are 'on' by making a true statement either out loud or silently within yourself. An example may be: 'my name is ...' and state your name.

As you do this, allow your body to move naturally either forward or backward. Moving forward is considered the direction for 'yes' in body swaying. This is because if you fall forward, you can put your arms out to soften your fall, which is preferable to falling backward and banging your head. This is why a backward movement in body swaying is a 'no'.

If you are in a wheelchair or sitting, the same directionality applies. If you are dowsing from a prone position, it is up to you to first establish if a feeling or movement of your head to the left or right indicates 'yes' or 'no'.

If you do not feel your body, head or energy perception move at all after making a true statement, go back and redo the five preparatory steps.

STEP 3

It may seem pedantic, but once you have established a correct 'yes' statement, it is important that you now also verify the directionality for 'no'. To do this, make a false statement. An example may be: 'my name is ...' and say a different name.

STEP 4

If you are content that you are correctly 'on', then you are ready to dowse.

Enjoy your new tool. Please use it with clarity and integrity.

Earthing/Grounding

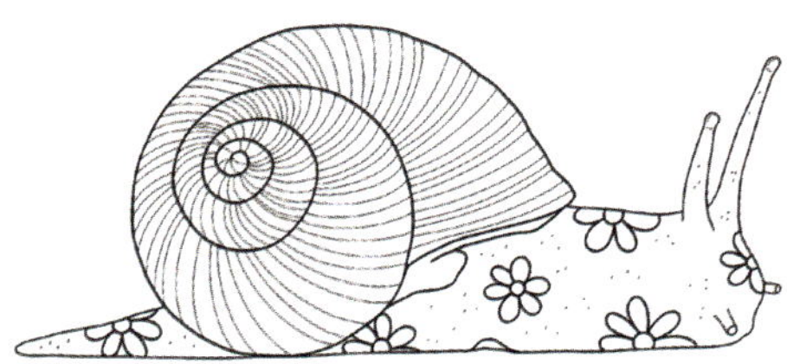

Have you heard the term 'free radicals'? If not, it has nothing to do with liberation. Free radicals are actually almost the opposite of freedom. When our bodies are healthy, our cells are in balance. When inflammatory conditions come along, they are a sign that unstable, electron-stealing free radicals have overwhelmed us in some way, leading to oxidative stress.

Our bodies are pretty amazing at fixing this by making the anti-oxidative stress compounds (antioxidants) needed to restore balance and, in doing so, health. Fresh organic wholefoods, adequate vital water, restorative sleep and non-toxic environments are some other gifts we can offer ourselves in support of our body's natural healing wisdom-ways. But, there is one other continuously renewed, and therefore limitless source of free electrons: bare skin contact with our beautiful Earth. This is called 'Earthing' or 'Grounding'.

How to Earth/Ground

Literally go into nature (this could be your backyard, a nature strip, the beach, the forest, wherever you like) and stand, sit or lie down, feeling the Earth against your skin.

How long and how often should you Earth/Ground?

Our observation is that this changes vastly, not just between people, but also at different stages for every individual.

Now that you have learned how to dowse, you can learn how to accurately test the length of time and frequency of Earthing that is optimal for you and those you love.

Some Earthing tips

DON'T GET COLD FEET

In traditional Chinese medicine, there are a number of energy lines called meridians that run through our bodies. On the soles of both feet is the start of an energy line that is connected with our kidneys. Though Earthing/Grounding is very important to health, allowing cold to invade this channel is not so helpful. We find that in winter or in cold and wet places, placing our heads or hands on trees or plants connected to the Earth is equally effective.

DON'T WEAR SHOES WHILE EARTHING/GROUNDING

If your footwear has rubber or synthetic soles and/or insoles, this will prevent you from Earthing. Leather is also non-conductive, and will only allow Earthing to occur if you have perspired enough to permit healing conduction between you and the Earth. If you stand with shoes on the Earth and hold the hand of a person who is standing with bare feet on the Earth, you will, through them, receive grounding.

MATS AND OTHER DEVICES

When it comes to Earthing/Grounding, nature is best. If this isn't possible, research 'DIY' Earthing devices.

REBALANCING AFTER LOCKDOWN

In terms of COVID lockdown impacting all aspects of health, this gift from our Earth is invaluable.

IN THESE TIMES OF CHANGE, GROUNDED MYSTICS ARE VALUABLE ASSETS FOR OUR WORLD

BECOMING YOUR MYSTIC SELF:

SPIRIT

Identifying and responsibly clearing stagnant energy

Have you ever walked into a room and straightaway felt uplifted or calmer in some way? Or sat down in a chair in a waiting area and started to feel apprehensive? Maybe you even started to sense butterflies in your belly?

Maybe you often feel a bit of swirling or tightening in your belly or throat? Or little surges of panic flaring up and bursting through your brain, making the world all of a sudden feel mashed and disorientating?

From the perspective of our basic five senses (sight, smell, sound, taste, touch), there most likely will not be definitive information obtainable as to why these sense perceptions arise. Many people have gone through barrages of brilliant medical testing and imaging devices only to be told that what they are feeling has no discernible cause.

Now that you have entered upon your mystic pathway, it is important that you understand stagnant energy.

Here is one simple tool you can begin using right now to clear and clean disruptive and distorting energy from around your head and body. Over time, you may feel like extending the application to your bed, your bedroom, your desk, your classroom, your home, your work-place, and so on.

Why it's important to clear your energy

Think of what can happen between your teeth when you have eaten mango from around the seed. Or when you have played sport on a field after it has rained. We are all educated about the need to brush and floss our teeth and wash our clothes, but very few of us have been taught how to clear and strengthen the energy space or auric field that surrounds us.

As you progress upon your mystic path, the importance and potency of the intent you hold behind what you think, say and do will have increasing relevance.

When clearing stagnant energies, you have options: you can clear from a belief that the world is hostile; that you need to armour up and protect yourself against attack or predatory forces; or you can clear energies from an intentional space of love, trust and strength.

The first option is highly non life-affirming and never recommended. Instead, always Centre and ground your intention from a space of personal empowerment.

This is a statement you may like to use (or just feel) regularly:

I stand in my Centre and cast no shadow.

If you were the sun, this is what you would do. Or rather, if you were the sun, this is what you would be. A being who radiates clear light in all directions effortlessly and free from all shadows.

Clearing stagnant energy

STEP 1: IDENTIFYING STAGNANT ENERGY

This first step is to establish if your energy system is clear or not. You can phrase this question in any way that feels right for you.

An example is to say out loud or silently inside:

"Do I carry any energies that do not belong to me?"

If the answer is a definite 'no' (no stagnant energies) or 'clear', go to step 4.

If the answer is 'yes' or 'not sure' (you feel you don't really know if you are carrying interfering or stagnant energies), there is one important thing you need to do before continuing through to step 2.

TRANSMUTATIONAL FIRE — ESTABLISHING YOUR WASTE RECEPTACLE

Just because energy may not be visible to everyone, it is very real and can have adverse consequences when it is released but not properly cleared. To transmute means to change one thing into something else. So before moving onto step 2, you need to first establish your waste receptacle. You could do this by physically lighting a candle, or through visualising or imagining a bright but tame ball of fire. These fire spheres can present in different colours at different times, so trust in what you sense.

You may also instinctively feel like using some other transmuting method which is totally okay. Some people may feel a guardian spirit arrive with a golden sack into which stagnating energies can be directed. Some may see a barrel of corrosive acid. Again, you are encouraged to trust in what you sense. Whatever is used, it's important that at the end of every clearing, you also clear away, in its entirety, the waste receptacle, and so, all that it contains. Blasting disruptive energies off our world into space or tossing them into water are not transmutational, they are forms of polluting and passing problems on.

Once you have established where you will direct all the stagnating energies, move to step 2.

STEP 2: CLEARING STAGNANT ENERGY

The upcoming statement may at first seem to be a little long-winded, but has been purposefully phrased this way to ensure there are no loopholes or concealing spaces where disruptive energies can linger.

With your transmutational fire or equivalent waste receptacle ready, say from a place of empowerment, internally or out loud:

> "I command … (dotted space explained below) that any energies existing beneath my highest vibrational level leave now back to the light or from whence they've come."

STEP 3

Take a long and deep breath in and hold for a few seconds before directing the breath and all departing energies into your transmuting agent. You may need to repeat this a couple of times. When you are ready and centred again, repeat the statement from step 1:

> "Do I carry any energies that do not belong to me?"

If your answer is a definite 'no' (you feel that you are now completely clear) congratulations. Please skip this next section and go to step 4.

If your answer is anything but 'no', repeat step 2 with an even stronger intentional alignment. If you do this with aligned conviction, you most likely will not need to repeat step 2 more than twice in any clearing session. However, there are some other reasons why you may still be receiving from yourself a knowing that you are not yet fully clear.

POSSIBLE REASON 1

If this is the first time you have ever tried to clear your auric field, there may be a bit of a backlog. As we initially established, there is no hurry and no time device measuring you. Simply trust that it is not going to be too much longer until you are clear and radiating as your own Earth-sun. It may be that there is a different process or tool in this book that you could benefit from utilising before returning again to step 2 (see the section on 'disentangling cords').

POSSIBLE REASON 2

Anything that has diminished your clarity and/or vitality has already used up enough of your precious life force.

Therefore, you do not need to concern yourself at all with what more stubborn or resistant energies might/might not be.

If you look back to step 2, you will see a dotted space following the words 'I command'. This space has been left to give you an option to insert the name of a spiritual power that has personal resonance with you. When you have forged a steadfast connection with your Centre, and on a cellular level integrated that this light is a source energy, you may not need to use this following tool. But before then, and quite possibly even after you have consolidated steady connectivity, feel supported by the limitless help that is available to you. All you need do is ask.

For example, in the dotted section of step 2, you could insert and so call upon the name of your Deity. You could alternatively call on back-up from a loved one who has passed over, your pet, a treasured plant or any other nature-based or mythical figure of light.

If you happen to be carrying any particularly 'lost' attachments that have forgotten or refuse to recognise light, including 'or from whence they've come' eliminates every possible evasion. So you can feel completely safe and empowered within this part of your path, dear mystic.

Always remember that despite what your lonely teacher tries to incessantly tell you, you are all-powerful and fully capable of clearing any stagnant energy, no matter how old or clingy.

STEP 4

Welcome and congratulations. Your clarity is a great gift. The final step is to now fortify your auric field.

Fortifying your auric field

The following process to fortify your now clear auric field is not a guarded 'no trespassing' energetic signature. Fortification in this context means strengthening. Again, repeating earlier information, this is because you will be doing this fortification from an empowered and loving space. You will be extending a field of light that you breathe out around your body. You may like to see or imagine it as an egg shape but highly luminous. Eastern practitioners sometimes refer to an aspect of this protective field as 'Wei Qi'.

It is important that you have made sure that your energy is clear before completing this final step. It is also important that you understand that like brushing your teeth, you cannot do this process just once for your entire life. You may like to think about incorporating it, or an adapted version that resonates better with you, into your daily cleaning routine. For example, you could practise this in the shower or in your car after work.

White light

Your heart space

Red light

FORTIFYING YOUR AURIC FIELD WITH RED AND WHITE LIGHT

1. Close your eyes and run your awareness down into the central core of the Earth. If your lonely teacher attempts to disrupt this process by inserting 'hell realms' or other ghouls, simply delete this imagery and reset your intention. See or feel a brilliant sphere of red light.
2. Send your awareness up as high as you can perceive. Trust that your will to connect with this luminous white light breaks all known concepts of space and time. Similarly, if the lonely teacher attempts to interfere, simply breathe the distraction away until you see or sense the luminous sphere of bright, white light.
3. Simultaneously breathe in red from the Earth and white from the sky.
4. Spend a few moments calmly breathing as the red and white lights unite inside your heart-space. You will soon notice that they begin to merge and become the most beautiful, almost other-worldly, frequency of pink light.

Take as long as you need in this step.

5. Only when you are ready, draw a very slow and deep breath. Utilise your out-breath to carry the light from your heart around your body in a 360-degree, multi-dimensional egg shape. Repeat with as many breaths as you need. Although the light in your heart was pink, fully trust whatever colour you end up breathing out to fortify your field. We often notice it transforms into luminous white and/or gold.

Note: the colours in this example are not fixed. The reason red and white have been offered initially is to help you gain confidence in your ability to see, sense and direct energy. We encourage you to adapt your practice to utilise those colour frequencies that your mystic self guides you towards. In our experience, dull colours, black, grey and brown are not life-affirming for this practice.

PARAMAHANSA YOGANANDA

A quote that beautifully sums up this psychic hygiene practice is from Paramahansa Yogananda's book, *Metaphysical Meditations:*

"No matter what causes it, whenever a little bubble of joy appears in your invisible sea of consciousness, take hold of it, and keep expanding it. Meditate on it and it will grow larger. Watch not the limitations of the little bubble of your joy, but keep expanding it until it grows bigger and bigger. Keep puffing at it with the breath of concentration from within, until it spreads all over the ocean of infinity in your consciousness. Keep puffing at the bubble of joy until it breaks its confining walls and becomes the sea of joy."

Sacred sphere of light

When you reach the section on using transmutational fire to disentangle cords, it is crucial that you feel safe and secure. In order to achieve this, you can begin practising now by feeling or seeing an impenetrable sphere very spaciously encircling you and your newly fortified auric field. Know that as you do this, there is an inbuilt intention that will allow only those energies of the purest vibrational quality to enter. Anytime that you are inside your healing sphere, you are 100 per cent safe, strong and protected. It is a sanctified space for one purpose only, your limitless self-healing.

The seven major chakras

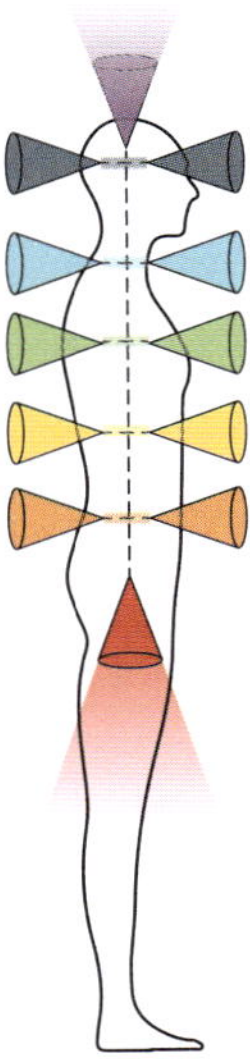

As you've already learned, one simple way to re-establish your balance is to go to your Centre and refill yourself (and every world) with the light from it. But, we understand that the illusionary forces of the lonely teacher can be tricksters at times, and so, can lead you into believing that being in your Centre is not such a simple thing to do.

Another reason why you may still be feeling overwhelmed and confused at times, or why it's hard for you to make or maintain contact with your Yom-point (Centre), could be from non-productive entanglements with other people's 'pain-bodies'.

To help you better understand the mechanism of how this can happen, here is a simplified guide on the energy field and the seven major chakras.

What are chakras?

In Sanskrit, the word chakra means 'wheel' or 'spinning disk'. Each chakra has a certain number of petals or rotating vortices. Each vortex metabolises a particular frequency or vibration rate.

Your energy field or aura is composed of different interpenetrating layers that are connected to the seven major chakras. It extends out from the physical body in a multi-dimensional egg shape. The energy vortices, or chakras, allow energy to flow in and out.

When functioning properly, the chakras absorb and distribute life force energy to your body via nadis (little channels). These nadis feed energy into the surrounding nerves, endocrine glands, blood, bones, organs and connective tissue. Their correct functioning is related to health on all levels.

The health and vibrancy of each chakra is governed by our strongest beliefs and psychological patterns. On a soul level, balance of the chakra system comes about through correct orientation and alignment with life. Whilst we are still under the influence of our lonely teacher (ego), there is benefit in focussing for short periods of time on individual centres in order to help bring about greater synthesis and balance.

As we grow older, the vibrancy of the chakras, and so our aura, tends to become dull and diminished. This is not inevitable, but more so connected to the lack of education about the necessity of clearing the toxic residues left behind by such things as negative thinking, unfulfilled dreams, old cords and trauma.

Now that you have stepped onto your mystical path, you have become a light-worker. With practice and humility, you will soon be able to not only help keep yourself vibrant and well, but also, when indicated, assist in the enhancement of wellbeing for all life in this world.

The seven chakras explained

Below are explanations of the seven primary chakras. When you get up to the 'Recording your mystic journey' section, you will find reference to an eighth point. This centre, as well as the alta major chakra, may become more relevant as you continue on your mystic journey. There are also other minor chakras at various sites, including to the sides of your eyes and in the centre of your palms and feet. Trust in your instincts and natural sense of resonance with these chakras. Be open also for this to change as you evolve and blossom.

THE BASE OR ROOT CHAKRA

- Governs the adrenal glands, spine and bones, legs, feet and toes and eliminatory system
- Is found at the lowest central genital area
- Can be perceived as red
- Is your Earthing and Grounding centre
- Aids your capacity to recuperate from stressors, illnesses or imbalances
- Reflects your belief about your ability to provide for yourself and/or family in terms of physiological safety and survival needs
- Is linked to your sense of abundance

THE SACRAL CHAKRA

- Governs the ovaries and testes as well as the rest of the reproductive and urinary system
- Is found just below your belly button (front aspect) and your lower back (rear aspect)
- Can be perceived as orange
- Reflects your sense of equality in relationships. The feeling of balance between what you give and what you allow yourself to receive
- Is connected with sensuality and sexuality
- Reflects your belief in your abilty to manifest creativity onto the physical plane

THE SOLAR PLEXUS CHAKRA

- Governs the pancreas, spleen, stomach, small intestine, liver and gallbladder
- Is found between the heart and belly button (front) and the direct oppostite point in your back (rear)

- Can be perceived as yellow
- Reflects your sense of self-worth and personal empowerment
- Is connected to the belief in your ability to assert your willpower positively and to think clearly

THE HEART CHAKRA

- Governs the thymus gland, the heart, lower lungs, all blood vessels (arteries, veins, capillaries), the chest and breasts, the shoulders, arms, hands and fingers
- Is found between your breasts (front) and between your shoulder blades (back)
- Can be perceived as green
- Shows your capacity for compassion, empathy, love, trust and forgiveness
- Reflects your understanding of interconnectedness

TRUST AND THE HEART CHAKRA

If we think or feel that our trust has been broken, we tend to shut down or put armour around our heart. We tend to think that we are protecting ourselves from future possible hurt. What we are actually doing is disconnecting from life and opening ourselves to the possible onset of feeling fearful, isolated and down. It is the magnetic radiance of the heart that expands the aura of the 'healer' and gives immunity from taking on the conditions of others.

It's important to know that psychic draining can only occur when the focus of identification is via the lower chakras (sympathy) rather than from the heart (empathy). An open and balanced heart chakra is what gives psychic immunity. It too allows trust in the future.

THE THROAT CHAKRA

- Governs the thyroid and parathyroid glands as well as the upper lungs, vocal cords, throat, neck and jaw
- Is found at your throat and neck
- Can be perceived as sky blue
- Is connected to speaking your truth
- Reflects the belief that your voice is not just listened to but heard

THE THIRD-EYE CHAKRA

- Co-governs (with the crown chakra) the pineal, pituitary and hypothalamus glands of the brain as well as the eyes
- Is found just above the centre of your eyebrows and the opposite place to this at the back of your head
- Can be perceived as indigo
- Is where we receive intuitive impressions and where we both visualise and direct manifestation
- Remote-seeing
- Needs us to practically act upon our intuitions

- Telepathy

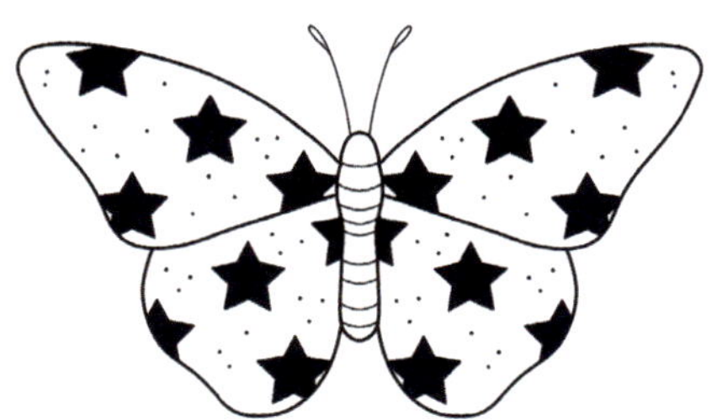

THE CROWN CHAKRA

- Co-governs (with the third-eye chakra) the pineal, pituitary and hypothalamus glands of the brain as well as the eyes
- Is found at the top of your head
- Can be perceived as violet or white
- Is connected with your openness towards Spirit
- Reflects your understanding and ability to hold faith or trust in 'the universe'
- Is linked with your ability to keep perspective on the bigger picture or 'divine plan', including the perfection of all timing
- Shows when the idea of oneness has shifted from being a conceptual theory into embodied reality

Clearing your chakras — disentangling cords

What is your bodily reaction to the above picture? Have you ever felt entangled by something or someone else's energy and/or problems?

When you have interacted with another person and have any residual, uncomfortable thoughts or feelings about them, it is worth learning how to scan and see if you have become entangled with any non-productive or draining cords or hooks from/to that person.

It is most probable that there has been no malicious intent behind any attachments that you find. However, there can sometimes be conscious intention within the entanglement(s).

It matters not whether cords have been consciously or unconsciously attached. It only matters that you learn now how to identify and clear them. Always remember, mystic, that it is your birthright to live in clarity and freedom.

Ways to disentangle energy

Hand mudrā

A mudrā is a symbolic gesture. Doing this hand mudrā can be an easy way of clearing external energy interference.

To do this, hold the source of interference in your mind, cross your wrists in front of your lower abdominal region (either physically or mentally) with your palms facing away from you until you feel the interference shift.

Remember: after any energy clearing process, it is always beneficial to use your exhalations to vitalise and strengthen your auric field.

Transmutational fire

Unless you have just opened to this page or skipped through to it, you already have a level of understanding about how to use this transmuting agent. If not, please refer back to the 'Identifying and responsibly clearing stagnant energy' section and refresh.

The main difference for using transmutational fire to clear other's energy rather than your own, is that you will see or feel the person you are disentangling from harmlessly on the other side of the transmutational fireball.

Note: please understand that if you have felt hurt by this person, within the sacred healing space that you have created, nothing other than your self-healing can occur. You can feel very certain about this. It is why we previously helped you to establish your 'sacred sphere of light'. Inside your healing sphere, you can feel totally safe, strong and protected.

BEFORE CLEARING

Before you begin clearing, cast your 'sacred sphere of light' as was explained on page 54 beneath Paramahansa Yogananda's joy bubble quote. Once safely inside, you may feel drawn to further prepare yourself:

- Stand straight with your feet planted evenly upon the ground. If you are unable to stand, endeavour to lengthen and straighten your spine to the best of your capacity.
- Ensure that your neck, jaw and/or knees are soft and not locked.
- Let your shoulders find their correct alignment and relax. If you can, physically lift and roll them or swing and twist your body from side to side with your arms freely flopping about. This movement is also helpful for healing your eyes. Become mindful of how the twisting motion not only frees up your spine but also stretches and flushes your liver/gallbladder (right side) and stomach/spleen (left side). Allow yourself to really feel the free and relaxed energy that is beginning to remobilise through you.
- Do the above point for a few breaths or until you feel more settled inside. Now, go to your Centre and shift your breathing into a cycle of three (inhale, comfortably hold, exhale). You can also do some 'hum-sah' breathing if that feels right for you. What you are doing is filling the central channel that connects the tips of each of your seven main chakras with clearing and revitalising energy. Remember: there is no time limit for doing this. Only when you feel ready, start your process of clearing and healing.

CLEARING YOUR CHAKRAS FROM ENTANGLEMENTS

1. This is one of the most important points for you to remember. As you shift old blocks and attachments out and away from you, a space is opened where these once were. Therefore, it is very important that you simultaneously fill these newly created spaces with the most luminous, life-gifting colour or light that you can perceive. This would be the same as a surgeon ensuring the correct dressing is applied to a wound so that it can heal quickly and safely. There is zero need for you to feel anxious in any way about possibly messing this step up or getting it wrong. All you need do is practise sensing or visualising this a few times so that you feel confident before you start your clearing.
2. Once you are calm and centred within yourself, with an infinite supply of luminous healing colour or light, start at your base chakra and look or sense what is connecting you to the other person.
3. If it looks or feels like the energy is clear and loving, it is okay. However, if you perceive anything but this loving clarity between you and the other person, use your out breath to dislodge the entanglement into the fire.
4. Completely trust whatever impressions arise for you. If you need tools, use them. If you need other helpers, ask for them to come and they will.
5. From step 2 in the section on clearing stagnant energy, you could again say the following:

   "I command ... that any energies existing beneath my highest vibrational level leave now back to the light or from whence they've come."

6. Feel supported by the limitless help that is available to you. All you need do is ask.
7. Once you feel that your base chakra is clear and freshly filled by life-affirming colour(s) or light, move onto your sacral chakra.
8. Then, at your own pace, move upwards, clearing and healing the front and rear aspects of your solar plexus,

heart, throat, third-eye and finally the single entry and exit space of your crown chakra.

When the clearing is done, and this may extend over minutes, hours, days, weeks or months, feel or see the representation of the other person return to wherever it is they may presently be. Then see or feel the fire, with all that old non life-affirming energy, completely disappear.

Drink some living water and be gentle with yourself for the next few days after clearing. Do not underestimate the enormity of this type of energy-surgery healing. You may feel you need to sleep more after and/or during this process. We urge you to go patiently but fearlessly, filled by the conviction that you have decided that you will be living the rest of your life free from all draining encumbrances.

The science of your Spirit — your mystic self

Hooray for you. By reclaiming and embodying the science of spirit that has been lost from the life of our world, you are officially now an agent for positive global change.

During these dynamic and potentially disorientating times for so many, the more people who consistently connect with their true Centre and stay grounded and clear, the better it is for all life.

Magnetic resonance, lore of attraction, psychic hygiene, defining your energetic boundaries, feeling safe and strong in the world; our prayer is that this type of education and information becomes available and taught to everyone.

We thank you, galaxies beyond ours thank you. Spread your wings and enjoy every breath of your new life modern mystic.

RECORDING YOUR MYSTIC JOURNEY

Beginning your mystic journey

We have left this space free for you to reflect on why you decided to begin your mystic journey. Is there a particular event, thought or issue that sparked your inspiration to explore your inner life? Your reflections may not come as words, but as before and after images or colours.

Befriending your Centre

Use this space to record in words, music and/or pictures, every detail about your inner altar, your Yom-point, the incredible Centre of You.

Becoming your mystic self: Mind

The lonely teacher

You may have heard of a teaching that is often attributed to the Cherokee Nation. It is about two wolves. One filled with anger and one filled with love. The Elders ask the younger tribe members, which wolf they will choose to feed.

Make a positive declaration here as to which wolf you will choose to feed — the lonely teacher or your mystic self.

On your mystic path, these words by Ramana Maharshi may be of assistance:

> "The degree of freedom from unwanted thoughts, and the degree of concentration on a single thought, are the measures to gauge spiritual progress."

In relationship to Ramana's observation, give yourself a score out of ten. Then set your intention to gradually improve your score over time. Zero out of ten would reflect that your mind always feels scattered and is filled by the noises of your lonely teacher. Whilst completing this section, make sure you stay inside a space of self-love, not negative judgment.

2022 **2023** **2024** **2025**

Quietening mind chatter

HUM ... 1, 2, 3, 4 ... 8 ... 55 ... SAH

In a gradual, safe and enjoyable way, record the length of time in seconds that you can comfortably hold your breath between HUM and SAH. Never force this and try to use your nose only for both the in and out breath. This practice of slowly increasing the time you can easily hold your breath is also a component of a breathing technique for helping asthma called 'Buteyko'. If you or anyone in your household experiences asthma, you may like to duplicate a copy of this page and magnet it to your fridge.

	2022	2023	2024	2025
APRIL				
MAY				
JUNE				
JULY				
AUGUST				
SEPTEMBER				
OCTOBER				
NOVEMBER				
DECEMBER				
JANUARY				
FEBRUARY				
MARCH				

Becoming your mystic self: Body

Take a breath

Take some time to just be. We are human Be-ings, not human Do-ings. Practise the three-step breathing technique and record a colour that represents how you feel before and after.

Revitalise with water

Do you feel you drink enough water to satisfy your body's needs? Do you find it difficult to drink water? Use the space below to write down some affirmations surrounding water. It could be as simple as: 'I am working towards being optimally hydrated.'

Thymus reset

Another gift Dr John Diamond left for us was his pointer towards the therapeutic quality of voices. He discovered that stressed tones, even on subtle levels, can disrupt not only the thymus gland, but also create imbalance in the cerebral hemispheres of the brain and a little bone called the hyoid that supports the tongue.

A voice on TV, or speaking with someone on the phone, can have a distruptive impact. We have left this space open for you to make note of names of people, situations, programs or environments where you realise you've been 'switched off'. In doing this, it will help you to build greater mindfulness. Then, over time, you will find that your clarity and strength have built to a point where you very rarely will 'turn off' under any situation.

On the way to that point on your path, make sure you keep tapping, smiling and laughing.

Resetting your vagus nerve

On this page, make a list of the songs or albums that you will always love.

Make some compilations and/or playlists. Next time you have to do house chores, you can be with the music that reminds you why you are alive. You may also like to check out Nāda yoga.

Dowsing — body swaying

As an application of this helpful tool, we'd like to offer you a mission. In Masaru Emoto's book *The Shape of Love*, a story is shared about Reverend Kato improving the quality of the water within Fujiwara Dam, Japan.

After sanctifying a space beside the dam, Reverend Kato then directed prayers from his heart towards two glasses of water before him, symbolic of yin and yang. Through the law of resonance, this prayer session quantifiably improved the quality of the dam's water.

We, like Reverend Kato, can together help restructure and purify Earth's water. There is great power in numbers. We would be honoured if you feel in your heart to join with us. Our sense is that your participation is a vital link in the healing and renewal of this world. Our world's precious water needs your love more than ever before.

Your mission: if need be, please go back to refresh on how to dowse (pages 40–43). Then when you are feeling clear and Centred, test whether it is in your highest good to spend one minute looking at a glass of water and sending into it your wish, prayer or intention—for all the water in this world to similarly restructure and return to its innate purity.

Record your feelings and impressions about your contribution to world-healing here.

Becoming your mystic self: Body

Earthing/Grounding

Your individually tailored Earthing practice is now part of your weekly diet. Make sure you are 'on', hydrated and feeling clear. Then dowse/body-sway in response to this statement:

It is optimal for me to Earth more than 3 times this week.

Wait for the response. Continue until you have the correct number of days for this coming week. Then make the statement:

It is optimal for me to Earth for less than six minutes per session.

Keep making clear statements until you can fill in your Earthing requirement for the week.

An example may be:

1st–7th
May 4/10 = 4 out of 7 days, 10 minute sessions

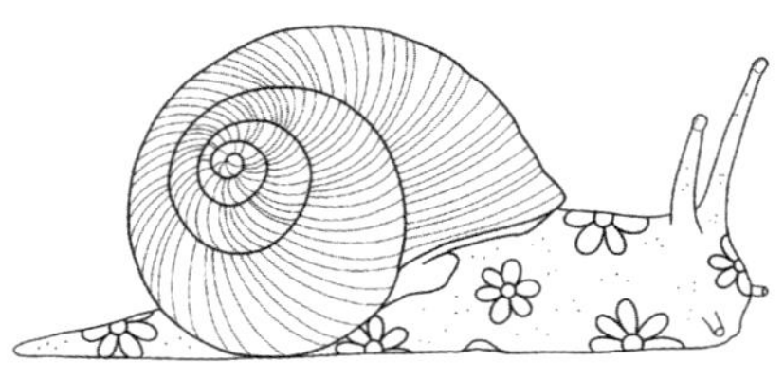

	1st-7th	8th-14th	15th-21st	22nd-28th/31st
APRIL				
MAY				
JUNE				
JULY				
AUGUST				
SEPTEMBER				
OCTOBER				
NOVEMBER				
DECEMBER				
JANUARY				
FEBRUARY				
MARCH				

Becoming your mystic self: Spirit

Clearing stagnant energy

Once you feel confident about identifying and responsibly clearing stagnant energy from your chakras and aura, you may like to apply the exact same technique to helping clear energy congestion from environments and locations beyond you.

If you just received a recoil reaction to this idea, you could ask 'who recoiled?'

Make a list of places in your home, neighbourhood, workplace and/or broader world community where you can sense energy congestion. Only ever do this when your frequency is clear and high.

As working together with others and/or in groups is synonomous with the now dawned Aquarian age, you may like to join with other like-hearted people.

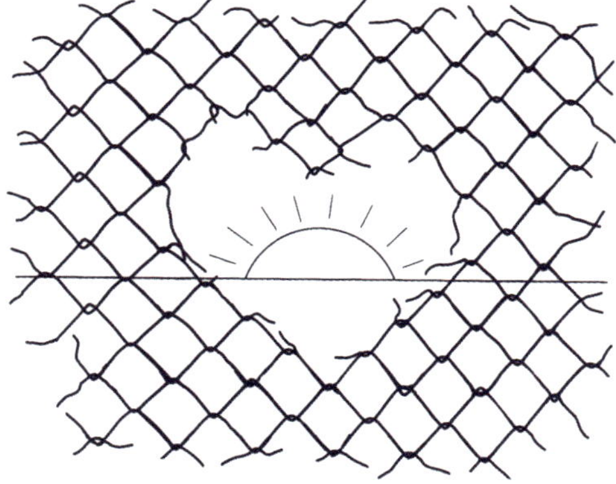

Fortifying your auric field

Wait for a time when you are feeling relatively calm and free. If you feel this is never, we ask you lovingly, when will you stop feeding that wolf? Centre and then send your awareness down into the Earth. What you are waiting to see or feel, is your new anchoring point. You will know it when you reach it, because it will fill your blood with beauty. Record your impressions here.

We shared Paramahansa Yogananda's 'joy bubble' with you so that you could practically use his wisdom teaching. Take some time to go back and read it again (page 54) and then come into your Centre. When you feel clear and strong, breathe your own joy bubble out into a place in this world where you know there is suffering. It may be to a friend or plant or animal, or it could be to a place overseas that is experiencing conflict and hardship. Record the symbol your heart whispers to you once you have finished. This extension of yourself, from an overflowing space of intelligent love, is the purest expression you can make upon your mystic pathway.

Becoming your mystic self: Spirit

The seven major chakras

Each chakra has a traditional name. For example, what you have learnt as the 'solar plexus' is known in Sanskrit as 'manipura'. It means 'city of jewels'. To help you deepen your relationship with your chakra system, we invite you to experiment with the sound and feel of these alternative names. We will share the phonetic pronunciations, for example: *manipoora* instead of *manipura*. You may not feel any resonance or attraction towards this section. If that is the case, please just move through onto the next page.

1. Base—*Moolaadhaara*—supporting root
2. Sacral—*Swaadhisthaana*—dwelling place of Self
3. Plexus—*Manipoora*—city of jewels
4. Heart—*Anaahata*—infinite sound
5. Throat—*Vishuddhi*—wheel of purity
6. Third-Eye—*Aagyaa*—perceive, command

8\. Bindu—*Bindu*—crescent moon cradling nectar

Although this appears non-linear,
it is where the bindu centre resides

7\. Crown—*Sahasraara*—thousand petalled

What colours, shape and size do you imagine each chakra to be? Draw or write your answers over the next pages. Then sometime around new year each year for the next few years, record your changing perception as your chakra petals open and shine infinitely brighter.

Base chakra:

2022 **2023** **2024** **2025** **2026**

Sacral chakra:

2022 **2023** **2024** **2025** **2026**

Solar plexus chakra:

2022	2023	2024	2025	2026

Heart chakra:

2022	2023	2024	2025	2026

Throat chakra:

2022 **2023** **2024** **2025** **2026**

Third-eye chakra:

2022 **2023** **2024** **2025** **2026**

Crown chakra:

2022	2023	2024	2025	2026

How I see my mystic self

Write or draw how you see your mystic self here. If you are a musician, write some lyrics or compose some music that may reveal to you how you see your mystic self. Use whatever medium sings through you.

BIOS

About the Author

A:ndrea entered the fields of energy medicine and structural re-alignment in the mid 1990s. Since that time, she has worked to help people clear pain and re-establish greater equilibrium in their lives. Completing studies from Monash at Queensland University of Technology, an ethics and human rights major influenced her post-graduate work.

Within her consultation and teaching roles, she draws upon this background as well as studies in astrology, numerology and Rāja yoga.

Peace here on Earth is built from people reconnecting with their own unique senses of purpose and peace. In this transition time from material crisis to spiritual re-emergence, A:ndrea trusts that you will, from now, begin focussing more upon what unites and connects you to other people and this world. She welcomes you to your mystic pathway.

w: y-om.com

About the Illustrator

Harper is a Melbourne-based tattoo artist with a minimalist, modern and clean art style. Born in the United Kingdom, Harper is a huge believer in manifesting and the power of the Universe. She has faith that the Universe gives us signs when we are on the right path and guides us when we are not.

Harper holds a Bachelor of Arts (honours) at one of the highest ranked universities in the UK. Throughout her teens, Harper explored many different mediums of art until she discovered her passion for handpoke tattoos at the age of 21.

Since then, Harper has taught herself how to tattoo professionally, securing her first studio job just nine months after starting. Harper tattooed for three years in London before emigrating to Australia, where she now works at one of the best tattoo studios in Melbourne.

Harper's work is romantic and feminine, exploring the concepts of love, emotions and inner growth. It is important to Harper that her artwork is created with intention and purpose and that she is connected to what she puts down on paper. She hopes that her artwork will invoke the same inner reflection for the viewer, too.

I: @harperrosetattoo

Other books in the Modern Mystic series

TRUE TAROT

Learn how to guide and interpret a Tarot reading with this fantastic handbook and Tarot deck set. Featuring easy step-by-step instructions, this book is perfect for beginners or a fantastic addition to any mystic's collection. Includes handbook and deck of 78 uniquely illustrated Tarot cards.

MANIFEST YOUR FUTURE

Learn how to manifest your ideal life with this fantastic guidebook and affirmation card set. Featuring easy step-by-step instructions and different manifesting techniques, this book is perfect for beginners or a fantastic addition to any mystic's collection. Includes handbook and deck of 78 uniquely illustrated cards.

NUMBER KARMA

Unlock the power of Numerology.
Discover the numerological power of your name and birth date. In this fantastic guidebook and Numerology Notebook set, you will gain knowledge on how to rebalance your number karma. Featuring easy step-by-step instructions, this book is perfect for beginners or a valuable addition to any mystic's collection.